D^ Kno.

REMARKS

OF

RICHARD H. DANA, Jr. Esq.

BEFORE THE

COMMITTEE ON FEDERAL RELATIONS,

ON THE

PROPOSED REMOVAL OF EDWARD G. LORING, ESQ. FROM
THE OFFICE OF JUDGE OF PROBATE.

MARCH 5, 1855.

BOSTON:
PRINTED BY ALFRED MUDGE & SON,
No. 21 SCHOOL STREET.
1855.

REMARKS.

Mr. Chairman and Gentlemen,—

The Legislature has been petitioned to address the Governor, for the removal from office of one of the Judges. This judge is a Judge of Probate, holding an inferior jurisdiction, it is true, and on a small salary, but the Constitution places all the judges on the same tenure, and what may be done to one may be done to all. The petitioners do not ask you to remove this judge without cause. In whatever form the reasons may be cast, the true and controlling reason is, that, as a Commissioner of the United States, he sent back a man into slavery. The petitioners submit the case to your consideration, and desire you to take such steps as the law and your duty suggest to you. The governing motive of the petitioners no doubt is that Massachusetts may do an act which shall both demonstrate her hostility to the Fugitive Slave Law, and punish a man who has executed it.

A number of citizens, yielding to none in their hostility to the Fugitive Slave Law, in their condemnation of the rendition of Anthony Burns, and in their fidelity to the anti-slavery principle, yet entertain grave doubts of the propriety and expediency of this course. These citizens, of whom I am one, have addressed a remonstrance to the Legislature, setting forth their opinions and their apprehensions. If this were a question between Mr. Edward G. Loring and the Probate judgeship, if it were a question between Mr. Loring and the Legislature, we should not have intervened. But it was truly said by the learned historian and able controversionalist, on my right, [Mr. Hildreth] in his address to you a few days ago, that this is a matter of public concernment, touching the rights and interests of all the citizens. We fear that you are in the situation in which you are asked,—

"To do a great right, do a little wrong."

And we believe the reply should be, still in the words of the great poet:

> "It must not be,
> 'T will be recorded for a precedent;
> And many an error, by the same example,
> Will rush into the state: it cannot be."

I had hoped, Sir, that others of these remonstrants would have appeared here to address you. But they have devolved the sole duty upon me. I must desire especially, then, Sir, to have it distinctly understood that I appear here merely as one of these remonstrants, only as a citizen, having a common interest with you all. I am here in no professional capacity, the counsel or attorney of no man. I should disdain to appear before you, on a question of state, to be determined on reasons of state, on an issue like this, as the retained counsel of any side or any interest. I desire to have it understood, too, that I, as well as the remonstrants whom I represent, am entirely disconnected from Judge Loring and his personal and political friends. We do not coincide in the doctrines of his remonstrance, or altogether approve of its spirit. My personal relations with him are slight, only those incidental to our common profession. He has never crossed my threshold, nor I his. And his peculiar friends have not been mine. I will go further, Sir, it is my own feeling, and I know it is that of some of the remonstrants whom I represent, that we should be glad to see one act showing that Massachusetts is in earnest; and merely personal considerations for a judge, who for his own benefit continued to hold another office, one he knew might require him to return a man into bondage, ought not to weigh a feather's weight against it. If we thought you could justly and safely grant the prayer of the petitioners, if we thought it consistent with the dignity of Massachusetts, we should not remonstrate.

Allow me to say, gentlemen, that there is one thing which should be clearly settled in our minds, in the mind of every one, before we can advance a step to the consideration of this subject. From the course of the discussion heretofore, I should apprehend that those who address you may be divided into two classes, those who reason upon the Constitution, and those who reason in spite of it. We hear a good deal about the people removing their judges, and the people holding the judges accountable to them. Some gentlemen reason as if the Legislature were the people, and the judges something else. They reason as if every limitation on the power of the Legislature were a limitation on the power of the people. The people of Massachusetts declare their supreme will, their highest law, in the Constitution. Every day they re-affirm this will. Recently, a year ago last November, they rejected all the amendments to the Constitution proposed. But every year, when they do not alter it, they re-affirm it. It is to the Constitution that we are to look for the voice of the people. The Legislature, the Executive, the Judiciary, are the several "substitutes and agents" of the people, having their respective powers and limitations of powers. The people are as the lord of the vineyard in the parable, who taketh his journey, and giveth to each servant his duty, and setteth the porter to watch. To limit the power of one department, or to defend the privileges or prerogatives of another, is not to limit the power of the people, but it is the people itself, in its sovereign capacity, apportioning its delegated powers, and balancing one against another. The people have adopted for their frame of government, a constitutional republic. They have acted upon the great and wise principle that the distribution of power is the safeguard of freedom, and the accumulation of power the essence of despotism. They have, therefore, distributed the great powers between the three departments, and they have intended each shall be, in the main, so far as is consistent with the ends of government, independent of the other. One of these departments is the Judiciary. Its ordinary function is to decide questions between man and man. Its highest function is to stand between the Constitution and the powers that be. Its noblest office is to protect the weak and the few against the many and the strong, the minority against the majority, those out of power against those who are in power.

The Legislature is by far the strongest department. It holds the purse and the sword. Its power of making and unmaking all laws, its numbers, its popular character, its public action, and its facilities for immediate communication with the people, its ready access to the public ear and public sympathy, are great elements of power. The Executive is strong from its position of command, its concentration of power, and its rapid action, and above all, as the power of appointment and removal is exercised now, from its patronage. The Judiciary is inherently weak. It is few in numbers, it has no patronage, the judges are usually elderly and retired men, they have, or should have, no political influence, and have many unpopular and odious duties to perform; and in public conflicts, decorum and usage enjoin upon them silence. The people have seen this, and have desired to strengthen the

Judiciary. There is another reason, peculiar to a constitutional republic, why the judges should not hold at the will of the other departments. The judges are to pass between the people and the Legislature, between the people and the Executive. The Constitution is made to protect minorities against majorities, to protect the weak against the strong, to protect the citizen against the ruler. Nay, the people themselves, having full power, have placed themselves under a noble self-restraint. They have declared certain great principles, and made certain great provisions for securing their observance. If there were no power to keep the Legislature and the Executive to the Constitution, it would be only a moral and not a legal restraint. The people have provided a department, a tribunal, for that purpose. That is the Judiciary. It is not a perfect safeguard, nor is it faultless, but it is quite worth our preserving. Patrick Henry said, "It is the highest encomium on this country, that the acts of the Legislature, if unconstitutional, may be resisted by the Judiciary." In England, Parliament is omnipotent. There is no tribunal to vindicate any right against the King and Parliament combined. A few months ago you had a Constitutional Convention in session here, to revise the Constitution, and recommend changes to the people. Imagine such a convention with full power to change the Constitution by its mere vote, and not obliged to submit its vote to the people. Imagine that Convention in perpetual session, and clothed with full powers of legislation, and you have a British Parliament. We have no such power here. Any man, however weak, however odious, has certain rights secured to him by the Constitution. If the Legislature, by accident or design, if the dominant political party, flushed from the contest, have sought to touch the hair of his head, he can appeal from them to the judges; and there is nothing on earth nearer Heaven, than when the judges of the land vindicate the right of such a man, against the popular sentiment, or popular interests of the hour. The great Lord Holt defied both Houses of Parliament in succession, in defence of the right of one man, and when he died, he had a funeral two miles and a half long, stretching out of London. If I were called upon to name the peculiar characteristic of modern, Christian, republican liberty, I should say it was the adequate protection of the few, and the weak, and the unpopular, against the great powers of Legislative and Executive authority.

Now mark, Mr. Chairman, the wisdom of our ancestors. While they declared, in the Bill of Rights (Art. V.) that all magistrates are accountable to the people, and (Art. VIII.) that the people have a right "at such periods and in such manner as they shall establish *by their frame of government*, to cause all officers to return to private life," they did, in their frame of government, declare that the judges should hold office during good behavior. The reason they gave for it was, (Art. XXIX.) "It is essential to the preservation of the rights of every individual, his life, liberty, property, and character, that there be an impartial interpretation of the laws and administration of justice. It is the right of every citizen to be tried by judges as free, impartial and independent as the lot of humanity will admit." For the ordinary purposes of trials, the mode of tenure may not be important, but in the great contests of political forces, if the judges depended for their existence, or their compensation, on the Legislature, their value as a barrier against legislative usurpation would be nothing. Accordingly, their salaries are secured to them by standing laws. Would it not have been a mockery to prevent the Legislature from holding their salaries at its yearly control, and yet leave the officers themselves at its mere will? I think we shall find, Sir, that, judged as all clauses in the Constitution must be judged, not merely by a literal and verbal criticism of the clause itself, but also with reference to the subject matter, the context, the reason and spirit of the whole instrument, the people do not intend that the judges shall be mere tenants at the will of the other departments. If it were so, what would be the value of the right that the judges shall pass upon the constitutionality of your laws. You have only to remove from office by address, the judges who differ from you, and you make yourselves the supreme judicature, and the final interpreters of the Constitution.

This question of the power of removal by address, is partly an historical question, and must be treated as such. It is derived from England. In England, the King has the power of appointment and removal. He appointed and removed the judges. The great object of the friends of freedom was to secure the independence of the judges. Why? Because they were to pass between the crown and the subject. After the revolution of 1689, the judges held office so long as they behaved themselves well. If the King was to determine when they behaved themselves well, nothing was gained for liberty. But official misconduct was a fact in its nature to be judicially ascertained. The British Constitution, too, had the ancient characteristic that official misconduct should be judicially ascertained, on impeachment by the Commons, and trial before the Lords. The true meaning of the clause, then, was, that the judges should hold until they were convicted of misconduct, on impeachment.

By the Constitution of the United States, the President has the power of appointment, and, by a construction too well settled to be disputed now, the power of removal. But it is provided that the judges shall hold during good behavior. Who is to judge of their good behavior? Not the President, nor Congress, nor both together. But, as all agree in the interpretation, it is to be judged of by the Senate, in its judicial capacity, on impeachment by the House of Representatives, two-thirds being necessary for a conviction. In the Constitution of Massachusetts, we have the same provision and the same construction, The general rule is, that the judge is to hold until his misconduct is judicially ascertained, on impeachment.

But the English Constitution still retained the power of the King to remove a judge on the address of both Houses of Parliament. This was not a power conferred on Parliament. Parliament has all power, It was a limitation on the power of the Crown. In our Constitution a similar provision is introduced. After the declaration that the judges shall hold during good behavior, it is added, "provided nevertheless, the Governor, with consent of the Council, may remove them upon the address of both houses of the Legislature."

This power is given in terms unlimited in the clause itself. The clause gives you plenary discretion. Does it follow that there are no rules for the government of this discretion?

The veto power is unlimited in terms. But if the Governor is to veto every law that he does not like, every law that he would not have recommended or voted for, as a member of the Legislature, he makes himself the supreme legislator. There are, in every instrument, clauses unlimited in terms, which yet are limited by the nature and spirit of the instrument, and by the context. Powers may be given, each unlimited in terms, which, if exercised to the extreme, destroy each other. Or, a single power unlimited in terms, if exercised to the extreme, may violate the declared principles of the instrument.

The pardoning power is unlimited in terms, But the Constitution declares that the Legislature shall make the laws, and the judges interpret them. It also provides that juries shall decide upon guilt and innocence. Now, is it not clear that if the Governor shall refuse to execute every law he does not like, or shall pardon every man convicted under a law which he does not like, because he does not like it, he virtually "suspends the laws, or the execution of the laws," and impairs the power of the Legislature? Is he to make himself the supreme juror, and set free every man for whose conviction he thinks he would not have voted in the jury room? Is he to make himself the supreme judicatory, and suspend the operation of every criminal law about whieh he differs from the Court? No statesman or jurist contends that, by the spirit and reason of the Constitution, he has this right. No governors have so interpreted the power. Yet the pardoning power, like the power of removal, is unlimited in terms.

We see then, that there may be limitations upon the exercise of powers, drawn from the Constitution. The conflicts of powers require these limitations. Whether you call them strictly legal limitations, or rules for guiding you in the exercise of your discretion, they are equally binding on you as statesmen, being drawn from the nature and necessities of the Constitution itself. True, there is no power which can revise your act, or declare it void, or inquire into your reasons. Nor can any person inquire into the acquittal by a jury, or call the jurors to account. But that does not absolve them or you from a legal or constitutional duty, which you are sworn to perform. Allow me to suggest some limitations on the removing power, drawn from the Constitution itself. As the fact of misbehavior in office is to be ascertained on impeachment, by judicial trial before the Senate, would it not be a violation of constitutional principles to remove a judge by address for alleged misbehavior in office, without trial? Still more, would it not be so, to remove him after he had been tried and acquitted on impeachment? Would it not be in derogation of the great constitutional right of every man to have the judges pass between him and you, if you were to remove a judge because he differed from you, because he held your law unconstitutional? If you were to remove the judges because they held the Maine liquor law unconstitutional, or the law for the annexation of Charlestown, and put in judges who agreed with you, would it not be a violation of the reason and spirit of the Constitution? Nay, more, would you adopt as your rule of conduct, the maxim that the three departments must be a unit, and make the judges your tenants at will, to resign or be removed at your intimation, reducing them to the condition in which the President holds his Cabinet? Yet, if you shut your eyes to all considerations but that of the literal construction of the clause itself, as the manner of some is, you will find a better right to do this in the case of the judges, than the President can find in the case of the Heads of Departments.

I trust, then, that we are agreed that there are limitations drawn from the Constitution itself. Indeed, I hope you have anticipated me in this argument, and that I have merely followed a course your own minds have gone over before. The remonstrants, then, may feel confidence,—may they not,—that you will not advise the removal of a judge, if it is to be done in derogation of any of these limitations. But, although some of those who have addressed you, have urged you to remove Judge Loring because you have an unlimited power, and need give no reason, yet that is not the ground on which the case of the petitioners is put by their chief advocate, (Mr. Phillips,) and I am bound to say that on the case as he presents it, I do not think that a removal would be a violation of the limitations drawn from the Constitution.

The grounds upon which Mr. Phillips puts the case are, that though guilty of no impeachable misconduct in office, Judge Loring has shown himself unfit to hold the office; that he has wilfully disregarded the will of the people, as expressed by the Legislature; that he has shown such a want of the judicial qualities, such inhumanity, such corrüptness of mind, and so forfeited the confidence of the community, and so incurred its permanent and just abhorrence, that the retaining him in office is a public scandal, and the public interests in the Probate office demand his removal.

If this case is made out, I do not doubt your right to remove him. Constitutional questions are grave questions. More than any others in the field of human science, they demand breadth of mind, reflection, experience, calmness and study. Yet there is no subject on which most men seem to think themselves so competent to decide, on which many men, and not unfrequently the most heated and the most inexperienced, are so confident and so absolute. I approach a constitutional question with more doubt and awe, every day I live. I would give no positive opinion, but I must offer you, in behalf of the gentlemen I represent, the best I can in the way of opinion or suggestion. I have read the articles on the removing power attributed to the especial friends of Judge Loring, and the language of his remonstrance, and of one, at least, of the public remonstrances. I have not been able to agree to the legal limitations there assigned to the power. I can see no limits to it, beyond those rules I have drawn from the Constitution itself, except your own opinion of the public interests. The possibility or probability of abuse is no argument to disprove the existence of a great prerogative. The power exists, and confidence must be placed somewhere. The Constitution places this confidence where only it can be placed, in the combined action of all the departments and depositories of power known to our laws, except the party to be removed. I have read the debates in the Conventions of 1780 and 1820, and I remember those in the Convention of 1853, and in their light, I can come to no other conclusion.

But in determining whether you will exercise this great, ultimate prerogative, you will be governed by certain moral restraints, by great reasons of state, by considerations of an enlarged public policy. You will bring to it a large discourse of reason, looking before and after.

As to your *mere right* of removal, I do not, as I have said, believe that your right is confined to cases of violation of law, either in office or out of office. You may remove the judge for insanity, or imbecility. If he has a permanent disorder which makes it unsafe or disagreeable to be in his presence, so that the public interests suffer ; or if he has so clearly and permanently forfeited public confidence, and incurred a permanent and just public odium, so that the public interests suffer, and scandal is wrought by his continuance in office, I do not see why you may not remove him. I put these cases only as illustrations, and not as limitations. I go further. The Bill of Rights says, (Art. XVIII):

> "A frequent recurrence to the fundamental principles of the Constitution, and a constant adherance to those of piety, justice, moderation, temperance, industry, and frugality, are absolutely necessary to preserve the advantages of liberty and to maintain a free government. The people ought, consequently, to have a particular regard to all those principles, in the choice of their officers and representatives: and they have a right to require of their lawgivers and magistrates, an exact and constant observance of them in the formation and execution of laws necessary for the good administration of the Commonwealth."

I do not know why you may not make these requirements tests of causes for removal.

But it is not what jurists tell us we may do, but what reason and experience and prudence tell us we ought to do, which should be our guide in the exercise of such a power. You find that from the beginning of the Government in 1780, until now, the power of removal by address has been exercised but in two cases, one being a confessed case of imbecility by reason of old age. Even then, it was used reluctantly. There have been judges who have held office too long, judges who have disappointed the public, judges who have failed in many of the qualifications which make them useful and acceptable, but the power of removal by address has not been resorted to. Why is this? It is because the public judgment has regarded it as one of those great ultimate powers, necessary to have in existence, but dangerous to use. The public see the danger that the medicine of the Constitution might become its daily food. They have thought it better to

——" bear the ills we have
Than fly to others that we know not of."

They have preferred to treat it as Burke has spoken of the unqualified veto power in the Crown: "Its repose may be the preservation of its existence, and its existence may be the means of saving the Constitution itself, on an occasion worthy of its bringing forth."

The history of political parties, the manner the appointing and removing power is now exercised throughout the country, should make us pause before we set an example which may tend to put the judges in the power of the majority. Has not the abuse of the removing power become the crying evil, the perilous disease of our Constitution? Has it not done more than anything else to corrupt the currents of public life, and lower the standard of public action, and heighten the violence of political contests? Are not all good men looking for some remedy, as for the very life of public virtue? Has it not rendered the President a monarch, and given him a power over the fears of all who are in office and the hopes of all who are out, so great that he is almost irresistible? If the power to remove judges by address had existed in the federal constitution, are we sure that the judgeships would not have fallen among the spoils of victory? We may say it would not be so in Massachusetts. True, our moderation and good sense have prevented it hitherto. But I can remember the time when it was thought an outrage to remove a postmaster, without other cause than his political opinions; but now, no one asks for a cause for any removal. Literary, religious, charitable offices, have, one after another, fallen before the march of party. Now, at each alternation of the annual municipal elections, the physicians of the insane poor, the ministers to the mind diseased, and the stewards and matrons under them, are driven in and out, almost as fast as the shadows that cross the twilight of the brain of the poor sufferers to whom they minister. Who shall say that if the taste of blood is once given, the honors and emoluments of the judgeships may not be sufficient, added to the acceptable doctrine that all must bow to the popular will as expressed in the election, to cause those offices to go as all others have gone before them? In a neighboring state, three whole benches of judges were once removed in the course of three or four years; and it is notorious that courts have been made and unmade to answer the needs of political parties. I do not undertake to say how great the danger is. We prefer not to incur it. I hold in my hand an article in the Evening Telegraph of last Wednesday, written by Mr. Samuel E. Sewall, as warm a friend of the colored race, as strong a condemner of the law of 1850, a man as little inclined to conservative opinions as any amongst us, in which he strongly remonstrates against this proposed removal. He says,—

> "Nothing could be more impolitic than to remove Judge Loring, for his obnoxious opinions, in the way proposed. So easy a precedent would be sure to be followed. The heroic judges of Wisconsin, who have nullified the fugitive slave act, in that State, might well tremble if a Whig or Democratic legislature was in power there, and adopted the idea that judges who held unpopular sentiments ought to be removed by address. If this principle be admitted, every Legislature in its turn would ostracise all political opponents within its reach, till the power of legislative removal became as odious and corrupting an engine of party despotism as the power of removing officers has proved in the hands of the President of the United States."

Recollect, Mr. Chairman, that this game of removal is a game at which two may play, and if the cry of "proscribe the proscribers" goes forth, it is not easy to see the end. I admit the right to remove for any of those disqualifications, the result of accident or fault, which make it for the public interests that the removal should take place. I will admit that if you make the removal in the present case, it will be in obedience to honest and commendable moral impulses. But that which is honesty with you, may be pretext with others. If you remove Judge Loring because he executed the Fugitive Slave Law, other judges, here or elsewhere, may be removed, because they do not. If you remove for what may be construed to be moral disqualifications, or for "flying in the face of the expressed will of the people of Massachusetts," as it has been called, do you not see how wide a field of exploration and discovery you open to parties less scrupulous, or more excited than yourselves? Would you desire to have each successive Legislature, in committee of the whole, revising the list of the judges of the land, and trying each by its tests of "piety," "temperance," "moderation," "frugality," and "fidelity to the fundamental principles of the Constitution?" Would not the evils of such a censorship be likely to be greater than its advantages?

There are then, Mr. Chairman, reasons of state, reasons of

political prudence, reasons drawn from experience, which will guide you in the exercise of an admitted power.

In the light of these reasons and considerations, to the force of which I know that you assent, I will pass to the less abstract, and therefore, probably, at least to the large audience that attends your session, the more interesting inquiry, whether a proper case for the exertion of this power, is now before you.

The causes of removal have been cast into form by the eloquent and distinguished gentleman who represents the petitioners at your table [Mr. Wendell Phillips.] And when I speak of his eloquence and distinction, I do it in no phrase of ordinary compliment between opponents. The bar of which I am a member, regrets daily the grace, the high bearing, the culture and the brilliance of eloquence which he has withdrawn from us. It is not too much to say that the public life of Massachusetts, rich as Massachusetts is in orators and scholars, regrets his loss. And when I hear of sacrifices made for the cause of freedom, of contributions to the relief of the oppressed, what, I ask, is the sacrifice of this or that office, or this or that preferment, the vulgar contributions of money, earned perhaps by compromises with slavery, to the sacrifice which he has made of the bright dreams of his youth, of professional and political distinction, of high station, and the reflection of new honors upon an honored name he has inherited, and greater yet, of the consciousness of leading a life of intellectual contest in the professional arena, before the public eye! All this he has sacrificed, because he would not misconstrue the Constitution. He saw in it a recognition of slavery, and his sense of duty, growing, he will permit me to say, out of a wrong view of the relation of men to the State, or rather of the State itself to the Great Lawgiver, this sense of duty called upon him for the great sacrifice, and he made it. Excuse me for digressing to pay to it my tribute of respect.

The petitioners do not ask for the removal of Judge Loring, because he acted as a Commissioner. Mr. Sumner offered to act as Commissioner in any slave case they would bring to him. But, for pretty obvious reasons, the claimants did not seem to prefer him. You would not remove him from his senatorship, if he had acted, and liberated Burns. If Judge Loring had liberated Burns, would there have been any petitions for his removal? Would this Assembly have met here to-day for his condemnation? It is not because he decided upon the case, but because he decided wrong, that he is to be removed. Now, Mr. Phillips is too much of a lawyer and statesman to leave the case on that ground. He fears that the sober thought of Massachusetts would not sanction it. He casts it in a different form. He says that this act shows him unfit for the office of Judge of Probate, and that he is to be removed, not because he decided wrong, but because he is unfit for the office of Judge of Probate. The apology for our ancestors in burning and banishing Quakers and Baptists, is that they banished and burned them not for being Baptists and Quakers, but because Baptists and Quakers could not be good citizens. This is felt to be a circuitous and unsatisfactory defence. Judge Loring has held his office many years in the public eye, and during the last year the attempt at his removal has been determined upon. Yet no one act has been brought against him, in his office. Does it not savor a little of artificial reasoning, of a technical conviction? Is it not rather a suspicious course of proof, to admit that there has been in fact, no misconduct in office, but to infer that there will be or may be, from a single transaction out of his office, the *gist* of which is a wrong decision? I should be sorry to see the condemnation of any man, still more of a judge, secured by such a course of reasoning and proof.

The strong grounds upon which Mr. Phillips places the cause of the petitioners, are two; first, that in acting as a Commissioner, he has violated the express will of Massachusetts; and second, that in the conduct and decision of the case, he exhibited traits of character which show him unfit for the office of Judge, and rendered him so justly odious that the public interests require his removal.

Now, Sir, I say here, as I said in the beginning, that the result of this petition to Judge Loring, is nothing to us. If the principle on which he is removed be a sound one, the question of fact, whether it was properly applied to him, is of less consequence. If the law is not violated, the question whether justice or injustice is rendered to him, is of minor importance. Yet it is well enough, while we are about it, to be sure that any man, however obnoxious he may have made himself, is not unjustly condemned. It is not beneath the dignity of the inquiry to be sure that we do no injustice on the personal question. Yet, on the personal question alone, I should not address you. But we all have an interest that a judge should not be removed upon any mistake or misconception of facts, however correct the principle; for we all have a deep stake in the tenure of the judicial office, and the immunity of judges from condemnation in all but the clearest and most unequivocal cases.

As I was present during the trial of Burns, and took part in his defence, and am personally acquainted with the principal transactions, I will, if you desire it, Sir, state my recollections of the events.

On the morning of Thursday, the 25th day of May, a little before 9 o'clock, I learned that a man was arrested and imprisoned in the Court House, as a fugitive slave. I went immediately in, and found Anthony Burns, in the United States Circuit Court room, surrounded by a powerful guard. I spoke to him and asked him if he wished for counsel to defend him, and offered him my services. As he is now free, there can be no objection to stating his reply. He said that it was of no use, that they had got him, and that if he put his master to any trouble or expense, it would be worse for him when he got back to Virginia. In his speech, recently made in New York, he says: "The lawyers insisted that I should have counsel, but I told them I did not think it would do any good, for what I had first said had crushed me, and I could not deny the truth, and my only hope was in the assistance of Heaven." (He refers to his having admitted to Suttle that he was his slave, in the presence of the officers.) Burns is believed to be a man of the highest sense of duty, and of a tender conscience, as a Christian. He was willing to contend for his freedom, and to escape if he could, but he was not willing to deny a fact which he knew to be true. I told him, if there was any flaw in the papers or in the proof, he would be released, and the counsel could take that defence. This he did not object to, but seemed afraid to make a defence, in the belief that it must fail and would make his case worse. Mr. Parker and Mr. Phillips both conversed with him, and they received from him substantially the same reply. Mr. Phillips will recollect the discussion of the ethical question, in which he and I agreed in the opinion that we ought not to induce him to a defence which he did not desire, even for his freedom, but should limit our efforts to ensuring him time and opportunity for making a free decision. Judge Loring came in and opened the Court. I went up to him and spoke to him privately, and told him the condition of fear and helplessness the man was in, that he was in no state to judge whether he would have counsel and a defence, and suggested to him that if he spoke to the man across the court room, with the claimant between, and the officers about him, he would be under duress, and that he had better call him to him, at the desk, and speak to him more confidentially. Judge Loring replied, "I intend to do so."

The claimant's counsel then read and put in the record, and began to question Mr. Brent as to the identity. I felt that if Burns was to have counsel he should have it then, while the examination was going on, and not after they had put in their case; for there was no one to object to questions or to keep the examination within rule, or to take minutes. I conferred with Mr. Phillips, Mr. Parker, Mr. Ellis and others, and rose and addressed the Court. I urged that time should be given Burns for determining whether he would defend, and to select counsel, and prepare his defence. I can say, however, that although I urged it with all my force, and I felt bound to do so, I had no doubt that Judge Loring would grant the motion. When Mr. Ellis addressed the Court on the same motion, I am quite sure I told him that, from what the Judge had said to me, I had no doubt he would grant the motion. It was resisted, and I regretted it was so, by the claimant's counsel. The reason, however, given by them, had its force. They said the man did not desire a defence, and had acknowledged the truth of their claim. Our only answer was that he was in no condition to determine what he would do. Judge Loring then had the man brought to him, at the desk. He spoke to him in a tone of kindness, and one to inspire confidence. Said he: "Anthony, do you wish to make a defence to this claim? If you do, you can have counsel to aid you, and shall have time to make it. You have a right to a defence, if you wish for one."

Anthony looked timidly round the room, and made no reply. I confess to you, Sir, I thought it was all over. Judge Loring said again, in a manner most likely to re-assure the prisoner, and putting his question in the most favorable form, —"Anthony do you wish for time to think about this? Do you wish to go away and meet me here to-morrow or next day, and tell me what you will do?"

We watched him anxiously. He gave a slight sign, but whether it was assent or dissent, I confess to you, Sir, I could not have told. The Judge seemed doubtful, but at length said, "I understand you to say that you would." Anthony said faintly, "I would." "Then you shall have it," said Judge Loring, and Anthony went back to the dock.

The question then was as to the time for the adjourned hearing, whether it should be the next day or Saturday. While this was pending, the United States Marshal went up to the Judge and whispered to him. Judge Loring, replied, aloud, "No, Sir, he must have the time necessary." The Marshal whispered again. The Judge replied, rather severely, "I can't help that, Sir, he shall have the proper time." He gave us until Saturday.

This is the history of the first day. We all know how subject we are to have our recollections affected by subsequent events. I have a habit, whenever I happen to be engaged in a matter of much public or private importance, to make a record of the events as they transpire. I find in my journal, entered either that day or the next, and before Saturday, a narrative of the events, ending with this observation:

"The conduct of Judge Loring has been considerate and humane. If a man is willing to execute the law, and be an instrument of sending back a man into slavery under such a law, he could not act better in his office than Judge Loring."

Now, sir, I am not willing to have my impressions at the time reversed and confounded by subsequent events. I know that not only then, but throughout the trial, I thought the conduct of the Judge, in the main, unexceptionable. And even under the excitement, the distress, the mortification of an adverse result, a decision which I thought wrong both on the law and on the facts, I am sure that no man ever heard me charge Judge Loring with an intentionally wrong judgment, or with a desire to decide against the prisoner. On looking at the printed report of my subsequent address to the Court, I find that I spoke of the Judge as having "counselled him in a parental manner, and advised him of his rights," and again of the "kind words" addressed to him by the Judge. Mr. Phillips and others think that I have mistaken the order of events, and that Judge Loring had heard the claimant's case, and would have pronounced his decision and sent off Burns forthwith, if we had not interfered. He gives to me the entire credit of preventing it. This is not my impression. I think my order of events is correct. Judge Loring needed not, and ought not, perhaps, to have heard the claimant's case before calling up Burns; but I have no doubt that he had determined to give Burns time, and to call him to him, but intended to require the claimant's case to be shown first. I am sure that I was not suspicious, at the time, of his intentions, and that is to me the best evidence. Indeed, I will frankly say, that if Judge Loring had addressed him as all other judges address prisoners, across the bar, if he had not called him to him, and in a manner and tone at once kind and assuring, almost urged a defence upon him, if he had not caught at a slight intimation of assent, I do not believe there would have been a defence at all. If it had not been a case of freedom, if it had been a mere money case, Col. Suttle would have had a right to complain.

It is said that Burns was kept in irons, while in Court. I think this is a mistake. I am sure he was not in irons when he came to the Judge's desk, and I am sure that if I had noticed the fact, at any time after the case began, I should have felt bound to call the attention of the Court to it. I recollect that either then or on Saturday, Mr. Ellis, in addressing the Court, on a motion pending, spoke of Burns as in irons. The officers shook their heads, and the Judge inquired, and it turned out to be a mistake, and Mr. Ellis corrected himself. [Mr. Ellis, from the gallery—That was on Saturday.]

The U. S. Marshal, after the adjournment, refused to let any person but me see Burns. I told him I was not his counsel, and was a stranger to him; but he adhered to his rule. I would not see him, at least not alone, because he had declined a defence, and it was generally known that he had done so; and I was not willing to subject myself to the imputation of putting him up to a defence and to employing me as his counsel; nor was I willing to offer myself to him, under such circumstances. I do not know that I would not, at the last moment; but not if any other mode could be resorted to.

Mr. Phillips, the Rev. Mr. Grimes, the clergyman of the colored people, who knew Burns, and Deacon Pitts, with whom Burns had lived, in Boston, tried to see him, but in vain. They came to me. I told them I knew that Judge Loring would order it, and wrote a note to Judge Loring, who was at Cambridge, stating the course of the Marshal, and my reasons for not visiting Burns. These gentlemen went to Cambridge, and brought from Judge Loring, on the back of my letter, a note to the Marshal, which I read, but which was given to the Marshal, requiring him to admit two or three gentlemen who should give their names and purposes, if Burns desired to see them. To this the Marshal yielded, and Mr. Phillips and the others owe it to this intervention of Judge Loring, that they saw Burns at all. They visited him and brought me a written request from Burns to act as his counsel, and I then began, in conjunction with Mr. Ellis, who offered his services, to prepare his defence.

You will remember that one of the worst features of the Fugitive Slave Law is, that the record which the master produces, is conclusive on the facts of slavery and escape. The only question open is that of identity, that is, whether the man seized is the man described. We examined the record, and could find no flaw in it, on which we could rely with any confidence. The legal questions respecting the admissibility and effect of such a record had been fully presented by Mr. Charles G. Loring and Mr. Rantoul, in the case of Sims, and had been over-ruled. We had little doubt that Judge Loring would follow that precedent. The Supreme Court of Massachusetts, and the Circuit Court of this Circuit had pronounced the law constitutional, and sustained the jurisdiction of the Commissioner. On the point of identity, there was no hope of a defence. Col. Suttle and Mr. Brent were present, who had known him from a boy, and the latter was a competent witness. Burns had admitted the facts in the presence of Brent and the officers, and he had answered in open Court to the name in the Record. We had no reasonable hope of a successful defence.

On Saturday morning, we moved for a further delay. There was great anxiety on the part of the government officers. The night before, the Court House had been attacked, and one of the Marshal's guard killed. The only reason we could give for our motion was that, owing to the order of the Marshal, counsel were not engaged until Friday afternoon, and we were not prepared to our own satisfaction. This was true, and an important truth, but in a case not involving freedom, it would not probably have availed. The delay was granted. Monday was the Probate Court day. The Judge said he could hold his Probate Court until 11 o'clock, which would be sufficient for the necessary business. He accordingly adjourned our hearing to Monday at 11 o'clock. We understood this was rather for our accommodation; and I do not think it was a wilful neglect of Probate duty, as it is now construed to be.

In the course of Saturday, an arrangement was made by the Rev. Mr. Grimes, aided by Mr. Williams, now of the House of Representatives, Mr. Willis, and others, for the purchase of the freedom of Burns. Col. Suttle agreed to release him to Mr. Grimes for $1200, and in the course of the evening the money was raised. I know nothing, personally, of the transaction, as I was out of town, but as I learned it from Mr. Grimes, it was in this way. It was necessary to procure the proper order or orders from Judge Loring for the release of Burns from the custody of the Marshal. The Marshal held him under heavy responsibilities, and of course would not release him on any mere bills of sale. He required the proper legal warrants from Judge Loring. At Mr. Grimes' request, a gentleman called on Judge Loring, and asked him to attend to the matter. He said he would do so, and met the parties late at night, at his office. He there drew the necessary warrant or other order for the Marshal, and at the same time, at the request of the parties, the proper paper for Col. Suttle to sign. The Marshal either could not be found, or declined to leave his office, and Judge Loring, Mr. Grimes and the others went to the Marshal's office. All supposed then that the affair was over, and that in ten minutes Burns would be released. But there they met the United States District Attorney, who objected to the release of Burns, in behalf of the general government. He insisted upon the case being carried through, to its termination. A discussion lasted until after 12 o'clock, when Mr. Hallett objected that it was Sunday, and declined to go any further. As the Marshal seemed to be under the direction of the United States Attorney, all further attempts were given up at that time. They were renewed early Monday morning, but fell through, and the trial proceeded. The petitioners' counsel take great exception to the action of Judge Loring here. They seem to overlook the fact that Judge Loring's intervention was necessary, and was requested by Mr. Grimes; and I am sure that his whole conduct in that transaction was looked upon favorably by the friends of Burns. I cannot doubt that if you will call Mr. Grimes before you, you will find that he so regards it now.

Mr. Phillips has testified to a remark which Judge Loring made to him at Cambridge, on Friday afternoon, when he went to get the letter to the Marshal. I perfectly recollect that when Mr. Phillips returned from Cambridge, he reported to me a remark by Judge Loring, which he regarded as discouraging, and which struck him unfavorably. I do not recollect the words, but the remark was in substance as he now states it. Yet I suppose Mr. Phillips would hardly desire to place the removal on a single phrase, as to which there may have been some misapprehension, or a failure to express correctly what was in the speaker's mind.

Now, Sir, we come to Judge Loring's final decision. I have said that we had no defence, except the points of law on the record. The defence we were able to make, arose from accident. If Col. Suttle's counsel had kept to the line of strict proof, put in their record, and merely proved the identity by Mr. Brent, we could have done nothing. They were left to do more. They examined Mr. Brent also on the points of slavery and escape. In this examination, it came out that Burns had been leased to Mr. Millspaugh, and escaped from his custody, and not from Col. Suttle's, and that he was in Richmond on the 24th of March. This course opened to us the legal questions on which we relied, and which I need not repeat here. It also opened the evidence on the identity, all turning on the date fixed by Mr. Brent. We showed that a man sworn to be the prisoner, was in Boston a fortnight before the date fixed by Mr. Brent for his escape from Richmond. It is not necessary to go into these points here. Judge Loring took two days to consider the case, and decided against us, on the law and the facts. I thought this decision wrong then, and I think so now. An article in the Boston Atlas, which has been alluded to, entitled "The decision which Judge Loring might have given," contained my views of it at the time, and I am quite as confident of their correctness now as then. I think the decided preponderance of opinion at the Bar is against his decision. Yet it is just to him to say that Mr. Phillips and I are both pretty well assured that, at least, one sound lawyer, who has distinguished himself by opposition to the Fugitive Slave Law, considered the decision inevitable. You would not remove him for a wrong decision. It must have been one so clearly wrong as to show him beyond doubt unfit for the judgeship of an inferior court, or to show corruption, or wilful error.

On a point like this, I would rather trust to a judgment formed at the time, than to one which may be warped by intervening events. It is for this reason that I violate good taste in referring so often to my own words. I find that, in a letter written at the time to a friend who sympathized with me, and thought the decision wrong, I said, "Judge Loring decided wrong — not from any corrupt motive, but from causes partly psychological, and partly accidental. This was a case admitting of, and, to some extent, requiring new applications or developments of fundamental principles, and Judge Loring has none of those strong instincts in favor of justice and humanity, which, followed by judges at intervals, in leading cases, have gradually changed the jurisprudence of England from a system of tyranny to a system of liberty; and the habits and associations of years, as well as his natural character, have led him to look chiefly at the interests of property, and the preservation of quiet and ease."

I think the true solution of the matter is this. If it had been a mere question of property, governed by the ordinary rules, it probably would have been decided against Burns. As an issue of liberty, to be governed by the presumptions and principles to be applied to such an issue, judges and juries, without conscious departure from duty, would probably differ, according to the instincts and temper of mind they might bring to the case. Judges had always allowed prisoners to sit in their courts in irons. Judges of average humanity acquiesced in it. Presently comes Lord Holt, with his intrepidity of character, and his strong instincts of liberty, and orders the irons off. Many judges of average humanity and intellect might well have allowed the claim of an Englishman, living in the English colonies, to bring his slave to England and carry him away again, as he held him in the colonies under laws recognized in England. But Lord Holt, not a philosopher or an orator, but for intrepidity, originality, and high instincts, the first man in the history of British jurisprudence, held that a slave could not breathe in England. With what travail and labor was Lord Mansfield brought to re-affirm the same doctrine in the case of Somerset, more than half a century afterwards. Philosophers agreed that the drop of water was an element, an ultimate substance. Then comes a man of original power, breaks through the conventional rules and theories, and cleaves the drop of water in twain. It does not follow that all who preceded him were grossly incompetent men. Recollect that the Supreme Court of Massachusetts, and the Circuit and District Courts of this Circuit, had pronounced the law constitutional. No man doubts that all the judges of the Supreme Court of the U. States would so hold. The vast preponderance of judicial and professional opinion in the country was in its favor; so much so, that Mr. Webster arrogantly said, that no man whose practice was worth £40 a year, thought otherwise. The public sentiment of Boston had sustained the rendition of Sims, three years before. Judge Loring had grown up under the shadow of Mr. Webster and Judge Shaw; he held their opinions and those of the judges of the other courts, and the opinion of his friends, Judge Curtis and Judge Sprague, in the highest respect. He was a man to receive the opinions, and to be much governed by the influences about him. He did not bring to the cause the high instincts of liberty and justice, the original power, the independence, which the cause required. The decision was the result of this. That is all that can be said about it. I find, too, that Mr. Sewall, who was conusant of the course of the trial, and took a deep interest in it, says, in the article to which I have referred,—

"Abhorrent to us as this act was, it is but justice to Judge Loring to believe that in performing it, he was governed by a sense of duty and official responsibility. His views of duty in this respect, no doubt, differ from ours as widely as pole from pole; yet it is not easy to see how they unfit him for a probate judge. Ought he then to suffer punishment for a decision which he regarded as legal, and felt himself bound to make? No person acting in a judicial or quasi-judicial capacity, ought to be subject to any penalty for a mere error of judgment, whether it regards law or fact. The judge and the juror are equally protected by this principle. To remove a judge from the bench because he has offended the king by his decisions, and to fine and imprison jurors for honest verdicts, shock us as exercises of arbitrary power that tend to prostrate all independence of thought and action in those who are subject to such tyranny. Whether the decision of the judge or the juror be right or wrong, he ought to be subjected to no penalty for it, unless his conduct has been wilfully corrupt. So it ought to be with the Commissioner."

It is fair also to Judge Loring to say that the public sentiment of State Street and Beacon Street, did not demand the rendition of Burns. It would have been better pleased with his release. The passage of the Nebraska Bill had caused a great change in public sentiment here; and the men who subscribed money and armed themselves to send back Sims in 1851, were talking high treason at the corners of the streets. A Whig President was not in power, and Judge Loring held his office secure, at the will of his friend and relative Judge Curtis.

Mr. Phillips.—We are not so sure of that.

Mr. Dana.—You do not think Judge Curtis would remove him if he had released Burns?

Mr. Hildreth and others.—We fear he would.

Mr. Dana.—I do not think so. Gentlemen are going too far, and doing injustice, right and left. I have always borne testimony to the absolute impartiality with which Judge Curtis tried the Rescue cases. I know his opinions on the legal questions, but I am sure he would do no such thing.

It is said that "public rumor" charges Judge Loring with having communicated his decision to the United States Marshal before he delivered it in Court. Sir, we must do justice even to our enemies. We are in danger of doing injustice here. I am quite sure "public rumor" is mistaken. On Friday morning, a few minutes before the Court was opened, I went to the Marshal, (Mr. Freeman) and told him I had a question to put him, which he might answer or not, as he pleased. I asked him if he had any knowledge or intimation which way the opinion was to be. He said he had not the least, any more than myself, and that he had been obliged to make his preparations in the alternative. He declined to tell me what his preparations were in case of a decision against Burns, but he told me what they were in case of his acquittal, and assured me that he had no warrant and knew of no intention to make a second arrest. I told him I should give my arm to Burns and lead him out. I thought that was the safest for Burns, and the most likely to prevent violence. I am quite sure, too, that one of Col. Suttle's chief friends, a Southern law student, from Cambridge, who was in his confidence, did not know what the decision was to be. Now, whatever faults Mr. Freeman may have, and he is a mere soldier at his post, and obeys the order of his chief, asking no questions; he is a man to look you in the eye and tell you the exact truth: I have always found him such. I would not select him for my judge or my clergyman, but I believe his word. I saw him again to-day, and he not only confirmed what I have now told you, but he added that the night before, he went to Judge Loring and told him his situation, the great responsibility he was under, the embarassments and risks of an alternative preparation, and asked him to let him know what the decision was to be. Judge Loring positively refused, and said that no man should know until it was pronounced. So far from Burns being hurried off, he remained in the court room nearly two hours, and in the court house about four hours after the decision was pronounced, and before the procession moved. There was time enough to serve writs of Habeas Corpus and personal replevin, if we thought they were of any use, or could have got an officer to serve them.

Such is this sad story. I have given it to you in the colors in which it has always appeared to me, so far as Judge Loring is concerned. I trust that the last faculty which shall leave me, will be that of doing justice to an opponent, that of discriminating in the conduct and motives of men whose course I am called upon to oppose.

The gravest objection to the course of Judge Loring, that which will probably weigh most with the Legislature, is in the words of Mr. Phillips:

"When Judge Loring issued his warrant in the Burns case, he acted in defiance of the solemn convictions and settled purpose of Massachusetts, convictions and purpose officially made known to him with all the solemnity of a statute."

The statute to which Mr. Phillips refers, is that of 1843, chapter 69, sometimes called the Latimer Law. I think the construction of this statute cannot admit of a doubt. The Fugitive Slave Law, then in existence, the law of 1793, required the use of the State machinery, that is, the magistrates and executive officers of the several states, in the rendition of slaves. The State machinery of Massachusetts had been used for that purpose. The case of Prigg *v.* Pennsylvania decided that Congress had no power to require the States to allow their judicial and executive machinery to be used for the return of slaves. Massachusetts then passed the law of 1843, prohibiting the use of her civil machinery for that purpose. This is the true meaning of the act. To give it the construction contended for by some of the petitioners, would be to procure a conviction of a Judge by a strained construction of a statute.

The passage of this law, and of other similar laws, I believe, in other States, was one of the excuses for the passage of the law of 1850. The South said, if Massachusetts refuses us the use of her State machinery, we will provide that of the federal government. They did so. The act of 1850 was passed. When this law passed, all the U. S. Commissioners in this State were also State Magistrates, and one was a State Judge. Mr. Sumner, who was a Justice of the Peace as well as a Commissioner, offered to issue his warrant and sit as Commissioner in any case they would bring to him. I believe he gave written notice to that effect to Mr. Marshal Devens. Mr. Curtis did act, in two cases, but no lawyer as I am aware, contended that he had violated the law of 1843. At the very first session of the Legislature after the passage of the Fugitive Slave Law, an attempt was made to extend the law of 1843 to the law of 1850. The first section of Mr. Buckingham's bill (Sen. Doc. 51) so provides. The bill was lost in the Senate, by a vote of 13 to 16. The entire bill for the "further protection of personal liberty" was lost. The same year, in the House of Representatives, resolutions condemnatory of the Fugitive Slave Law of 1850, (House Doc. 187) very moderate in their character, were lost by a vote of 164 to 167. This was in the Coalition Legislature. The same year, during the session of the Legislature, under its very eye, occurred the rendition of Sims. The Court House was in chains. The judges went under them. The Sheriff refused to serve your precepts. Massachusetts law was suspended. Your Courts were closed to all, except such as the United States Marshal chose to admit. Massachusetts lay at the foot of the slave power. What did the Legislature do? Nothing! Absolutely nothing! Your Committee examined the parties and reported the facts. They complained that Mr. Hallett and Mr. Tukey insulted them, but said that the others were very polite. The Report was allowed to go by, and Massachusetts did nothing. The popular elections, even, did not indicate that Massachusetts was in earnest in condemning the Fugitive Slave Law.

In 1852, Mr. Sewall introduced his bill "further to protect personal liberty." (Sen. Doc. 76.) It passed the Senate by a vote of 18 to 16; but it was lost in the House, by a vote of 158 to 167, and its death-blow was given to it on the motion of Mr. Henry J. Gardner, of Boston. Now you propose to address the same Mr. Gardner, in his capacity as Governor, and ask him to remove Judge Loring from office, because he has flown in the face of the legislation of Massachusetts! In the same year, resolutions carefully drawn and moderate in their character, generally attributed to Mr. Hoar of Worcester, intended to commit Massachusetts against the Fugitive Slave Law, were defeated by a vote of 178 to 162. In 1853, Massachusetts elected Mr. Everett to the Senate of the United States, a man thoroughly committed to the support of the Fugitive Slave Law. And now, in 1855, this very Committee is reporting a bill, the first section of which proposes to extend the act of 1843 to the law of 1850, to do what Massachusetts has refused to do up to this time.

Now, Mr. Chairman and gentlemen, I put it to you, as men of candor, I put it to every petitioner in this hall,—has the Legislature of Massachusetts done anything to condemn the Fugitive Slave Law, since its passage? Has she not rather refused to do so? Do you forget the condition of the two great parties of this country, from 1850 to 1854? Do you forget the proscriptive resolutions, the erection of that law into a constitutional compact, by both the parties? Do you forget the condition of the Whig party in Massachusetts? Do you forget the overpowering influence of Mr. Webster? Do you forget how, after a few struggles of a reluctant nature, how completely it was

———" subdued,"
" Even to the very quality of its lord?"

Am I, are we, of the Free Soil party, to forget what we have said to the people of Massachusetts, that the unfaithfulness of the two great parties, made the existence of a third party necessary? Ah, no, sir! So far from flying in the face of the legislative will of Massachusetts, I fear Judge Loring has acted too much in accordance with it.

Mr. Chairman, it is high time that I brought to a close these remarks in which you have so long and so patiently indulged me. Let us review calmly the whole field. Judge Loring has not, by acting as commissioner, violated the law of 1843. To hold that he has, would be giving the law a forced and unwarrantable construction, a construction not put upon it by any Legislature, or by your magistrates, or by either the supporters or opponents of the Fugitive Slave Law, a construction practically denied by Mr. Buckingham's movement in 1851, and by the bill you are about to introduce. He has not flown in the face of the legislative will of Massachusetts. On the contrary, I am ashamed to say, he has acted in conformity with it. Now, sir, would it be dignified, would it be altogether chivalrous in Massachusetts, standing as she does upon the record, with her history of the last five years before her, having submitted to the insults of South Carolina, having been bearded in her own courts by the slave power, having been afraid to do one legislative act, or even to offer the vain oblation of one legislative resolution, would it be quite the part of dignity and gallantry for her, the moment she feels a little returning strength and security, to turn round and strike down one of her own citizens, a powerless man, who followed but too closely her own lead? I call him a powerless man. He is so. Who is more powerless than a man who has made himself unpopular? Who more powerless than a man who carries with him the consciousness of having been the means, the instrument, of such a result as the returning to bondage a man who had escaped into a free land? Much has been said about his powerful friends. His phalanx of peculiar friends and supporters, who have thrown themselves about him, doing his cause, in my opinion, more harm than good, whose generic name has become famous, have considerable influence within certain business and social circles in the capital, but that, I think, has been somewhat exaggerated. Beyond these circles, in the State at large, they are powerless. They are worse than powerless, they are exceedingly unpopular. Their support is an injury, and their patronage a disparagement. A public sentiment is arising which threatens to destroy the influence of those who made themselves active in the defence and execution of the late Fugitive Slave Law. No Sir, let Massachusetts first put herself right upon the record. Let her lay a foundation on which she has a right to stand. Let her entitle herself to throw the first stone, and pluck out the mote. Let her declare her legislative will, as she has not yet done, that her magistrates shall not be commissioners under the law of 1850, and let Judge Loring choose on that day which he will serve. You have as much right to do that, as you have to say that your Chief Justice shall not be a captain in the United States army. Let her declare that neither her civil nor her military machinery shall be used for the execution of the Fugitive Law of 1850. Then, if one of your magistrates shall offend against you, cut him off, and cast him from you. You will be in a position to do it with dignity, as regards yourselves, and in justice, as regards him.

I would end as I began. As between Mr. Edward Greely Loring and the office he holds, we have nothing to say. We desire to see Massachusetts condemn, in any way she can with dignity and prudence, the course of a magistrate of hers, who voluntarily retains and executes an office, which, with his views of the law of 1850, he knew might, and probably would, require him to re-enslave an escaped bondman. We do not think that Judge Loring has violated any law of Massachusetts. We regret we cannot say that he has. We do not see in his conduct in the office of Commissioner, evidence of such a state of heart and head, as makes it expedient to remove him from a judicial office in Massachusetts, to rouse the slumbering lion of the Constitution, to invoke that great ultimate prerogative, which neither we nor our fathers have exercised. We respectfully ask you to place Massachusetts right upon the record, so that she can act with dignity and justice hereafter. We take the liberty to suggest to you, even, that you may condemn the course of Judge Loring, in your report, for acting as Commissioner at all, while he wore the judicial ermine of Massachusetts, though it was not in law forbidden him. You may say to him, if you choose, "We cannot strike you down with the weapon which the petitioners offer to our hand, therefore go in peace." This would be no triumph to him. Say to the petitioners, "we deeply sympathize in the feeling which brings you here. We shall be governed by the same feeling in our future action, but we do not think it prudent, looking to all time, and to the rights and interests of all men, we do not think it consistent with our dignity to enter upon the course you have opened to us." The remonstrants believe that, in so doing, you will best preserve the proper independence of your judges, and the proper balance of your Constitution, which you are bound to regard. These are motives to influence you. We have another motive, which, in regulating our action, has co-operated with these. We fear that this step will involve the anti-slavery men of Massachusetts in a needless and doubtful issue, which they may live to regret; while we believe the course we recommend will secure the respect of all, and an ultimate ascendency to a sound and wholesome sentiment of liberty in the Commonwealth.

www.ingramcontent.com/pod-product-compliance
Lightning Source LLC
LaVergne TN
LVHW011139110826
845150LV00008B/2407

* 9 7 8 1 4 1 8 1 9 3 0 6 5 *